CW00550812

A PORTRAIT OF HACKNEY

A PORTRAIT OF HACKNEY

by Zed Nelson

HOXTON MINI PRESS

Book One
I've Lived in East London for 86½ Years

Book Two
East London Swimmers

Book Three
A Portrait of Hackney

To order books, collector's editions and signed prints please go to:

www.hoxtonminipress.com

East London Photo Stories

Book Three

HACKNEY – A TALE OF TWO CITIES

On a spring evening in April 2010, a 16-year-old schoolgirl was killed by a gunshot fired through the window of a fast food restaurant in Hackney. The gunman, 21 years old and riding a bicycle, was trying to scare a rival youth gang. On the same day, two men on a motorbike shot at two males walking along the street, who then returned fire.

It didn't bode well for the approaching 2012 Olympics. But Hackney – though crime-ridden, poor and dilapidated – was nevertheless in the process of becoming one of London's trendiest neighbourhoods.

Down the road from the shootings, contemporary design studios and modernist apartment blocks now pepper the landscape, like out-of-place totems of middle-class gentrification.

The social landscape for an underprivileged teenager growing up in Hackney, one of London's poorest boroughs, is a million light-years away from the new urban hipsters who frequent the cool bars and expensive cappuccino cafés springing up in the same streets. These worlds co-exist side-by-side but entirely separate, creating bizarre juxtapositions of wealth and poverty, aspiration and hopelessness.

This series, a work in progress, meditates on the confusion of cultures, clash of identities and the beauty and ugliness that co-exist in the borough today.

GROWING UP IN HACKNEY

I was born in Uganda, East Africa, but from the age of three Hackney has been my home.

I went to a forward-thinking experimental primary school in East London that encouraged art and independent thought, until my parents, as 70s hippies, plucked me out of school and took me and my sister on a one-year road trip to India, travelling overland from Britain in a diesel truck.

When we returned I had the misfortune of ending up at an extremely rough comprehensive school. I found out years later it had the worst academic record of any school in the capital and in subsequent years was closed down. It was set on a concrete landscape with not a blade of grass in sight. The school was encircled by housing estates and chain-link fences. It was not a place of learning, but more of survival.

Over the next few years I pierced my ears, shaved my head into a mohican, got a tattoo, was arrested for smoking dope, took acid in Abney Park Cemetery and buzzed around the streets in a motorbike gang. We were hardly Hells Angels though, we were so young we were restricted to 100cc motorcycles with L-plates. Most of the time it was harmless fun, but it turned dark. One friend became addicted to heroin and was murdered in a squat, another was badly injured in a motorbike accident, and another sent to jail for GBH after a fight got out of hand. Basically, I was the product of a bad inner city education, with the kind of friends that go with it.

At the age of 18, photography gave me a passport back to civilization, and the minute I started college I remembered there was so much more to do. I have since travelled widely through my photographic work, but remained living in Hackney and am watching with fascination as the area goes through a metamorphosis.

There's a recurring motif in these images of Hackney, of cracked pavements and walls, melting tarmac, and weeds and roots bursting through concrete. It is as if nature is trying to reclaim the land, and Hackney – under-funded, neglected and poorly maintained – is constantly being sucked back into the earth. It amuses me to see this, as I find other, wealthier areas where nature has been conquered depressing and disconcerting – covered over in tarmac, cemented and de-weeded.

In the run up to the Olympics, the artist Anish Kapoor said of his controversial red steel Olympic sculpture 'The Orbit', "It's a series of discrete events tied together."

I think that sums up my series on Hackney ... 'a series of discrete events tied together'. To try and make sense of the place seems futile. Hackney is a socially, ethnically diverse melee. It has violence, beauty, wildlife, concrete wastelands, poverty and affluence jumbled together, all vying for space. It is tattered and fractured, but very alive.

Zed Nelson, 2014

"You can't expect men of my generation to grow up. We're never going to be the men your fathers are."

Haggerston Park

*"We had a guy come in and try to buy
a cupcake with a fifty pound note."*

Tina's café

*"They just assumed the money
came with the fame."*

Kingsland Road

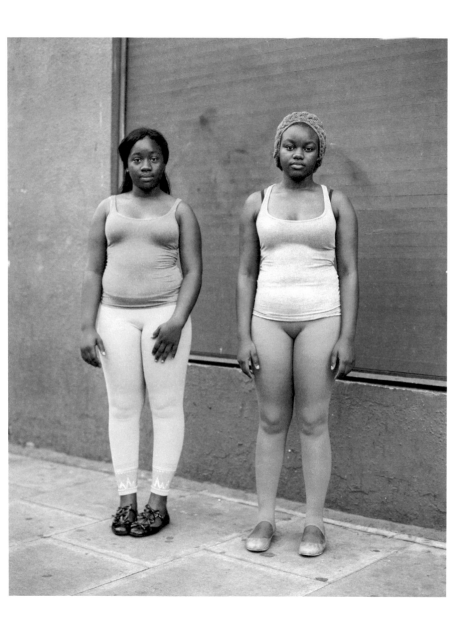

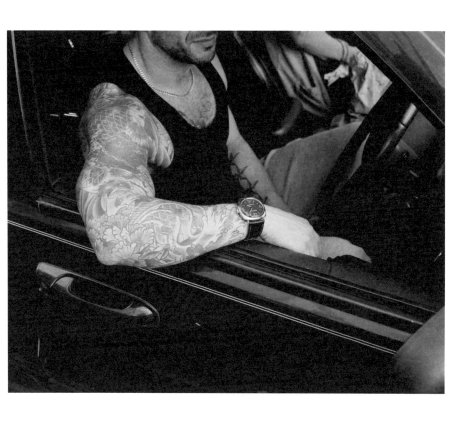

"Don't listen to them dude, I think "Nonchalance" is a cool name for a magazine."

London Fields

"He's a bit of a wanker, but I've got a horrible feeling he's the future. I'm meeting him on Monday."

Broadway Market

"It was the best of times, it was the worst of times, it was the age of wisdom, it was the age of foolishness, it was the epoch of belief, it was the epoch of incredulity, it was the season of Light, it was the season of Darkness, it was the spring of hope, it was the winter of despair, we had everything before us, we had nothing before us, we were all going direct to Heaven, we were all going direct the other way ..."

A Tale of Two Cities, Charles Dickens (1812—1870)

A Portrait of Hackney
Second Edition

Copyright © Zed Nelson 2014. All rights reserved.

Photography by Zed Nelson
Design and layout by Friederike Huber
Series design by breadcollective.co.uk

A CIP catalogue record for this book is available from the British Library.

ISBN: 978-0-9576998-3-0

First published in the United Kingdom in 2014 by Hoxton Mini Press

No part of this publication may be reproduced, stored in a retrieval system,
or transmitted in any form or by any means, electronic, mechanical,
photocopying, recording or otherwise, without the prior written permission
of the copyright owner.

Printed and bound by: WKT, China

To order books, collector's editions and signed prints please go to
www.hoxtonminipress.com